Consultant: Gussie Hearsey

© 1989 Blackbird Design

First published 1989 exclusively for
Mothercare U.K. Ltd by Walker Books Ltd
87 Vauxhall Walk, London SE11 5HJ

First printed 1989
Printed in Italy by L.E.G.O., Vicenza

ISBN 0-7445-1243-3

VISITING
the new baby

Bob Graham

MOTHERCARE · WALKER BOOKS

Edward and Wendy Arnold are
dressed up as Bat King and
Wonderwoman.

They are going to the hospital
to see their new baby brother
for the first time.

Edward is very excited. He has
brought his two best toys.

They are presents for the new
baby, Walter.

But baby Walter looks like he
won't need toys for some time.

He is very small, and pink, and
fast asleep.

"He's like a toy," says Wendy.

"Will he wake up?"

"Such tiny hands," says Dad, "and he looks like Edward."

"Where *is* Edward?"
"He's hiding under the bed with
his silly presents," says Wendy.

"Come up, Edward. Come and
meet Walter . . . and bring your
presents with you."

"They're much too big for baby
Walter," says Wendy.

"They're your best toys! That's
kind of you, Edward," says Mum.

"And I'm sure Walter will look
at them when he wakes up."

"Would you like to hold your
new brother?" asks Mum.
"He looks like he might break,"
says Edward.

"He's still asleep," says Wendy.
Edward is saved by the bell!
It's time to go home.

"Are you quite sure you didn't
want to hold him?" asks Dad.

"When he comes home," says
Edward. "I'll try him when
he comes home."